The Trader Joe's Easy Cook Cookbook
Cheap, Healthy, Hassle Free Meals
That Will Save You Time And Money!

By Rachael Ray McDouglas and Larry Recipes

Copyright Information

Copyright © The Trader Joe's Easy Cook
Cookbook

This Kindle edition book is a premium edition
2013. Created and designed in the United
States of America.

Table of Contents

Pineapple Express Burger - $3.24 - 50

As Directed Meals - 51

Breakfast

Quick Cinnamon Raisin Oatmeal - $1.08 - 53

Egg in a Frame - $0.52 - 54

Dunkin Donuts Big N' Toasty - $1.94 - 56

Waffle Berry Sandwich - $0.97 - 58

Almond Protein Shake - $1.22 - 59

Brown Sugar Bacon - $1.62 - 60

Desserts

Joe-Joe Truffles - $0.44 - 61

Easy Peanut Butter Cookies - $0.31 - 63

Two Ingredient Chocolate Mousse - $1.50 - 65

No-Bake Berry Cheesecake - $0.85 - 66

Banana Roll-Ups - $0.37-$0.40 - 68

Why You Should Buy And Read This Cookbook, A Brief Overview

Who is this cookbook for?
This cookbook is for you! Not convinced?
Here's a quick list of traits of people who will be interested in what we have to offer:

- You're looking to cut down on food costs in your budget
- You don't want to spend all night preparing a meal
- You need to feed one or two people at a time
- You don't have all the equipment lots of cookbooks require
- You live within relative proximity to a Trader Joe's
- You're a great person who is great

There are plenty of cookbooks out there with long prep times, tons of ingredients, difficult knife skills and resulting meals that feed an Irish Catholic family. If that's what you want – then look elsewhere. But if you want simple, quick, cost effective meals for one or two (though they are easily expandable for more people if needed) – you've come to the right place.

It's Cost Effective

Americans are spending an average of $151 a week on food (Gallup Poll, 2012). Figuring people average 21 meals a week, that's about $7.20 a meal, and just under $8,000 a year! That may be fine for the doctors and lawyers among us, but for the other 99% - there has gotta be a cheaper way.

The average cost per meal in our cookbook is $3.00. That means if you ate our recipes, one week of food shopping would cost you $63! Your annual food costs would drop by $5,000. Even if you splurged and ate out with friends a few times a month – you're gonna be coming out ahead. Way ahead.

Every one of our recipes is broken down by cost per serving (even by ingredient), so you know exactly what you're looking at in terms of the bottom line. Using our cookbook, you'll never find yourself at the checkout with the items for some Pinterest recipe only to realize the total cost is the same as your last month's salary!

Everything You Need Is At One Store

Sure we love Trader Joe's, and that's the main reason we based our cookbook around their store. But beyond that, most other cookbooks will send you all over town trying to find some bizarre spice or unusual noodle shape or god knows what else. Life is busy, it's hard enough to find the time to get to one grocery store per week – no one needs to be going to two more. That's crazy.

No Crazy Cooking Skills Are Required
You don't have to be a master iron chef to follow our directions. You won't be slicing and dicing and peeling and wheeling. You'll be preheating, combining, and stirring. Trust us, you can handle it.

It Will Save You Time
Not only will you only be shopping at one store, from prep to eating at the dinner table – most of our recipes will take you less than 10 minutes. We know what it's like. You get home from work at 6:00. You usually go to bed by 10:00. That means you have 4 hours of your day to actually do what you want (unless you have some incredible job). Don't waste an hour or two of it at the stove – there are way more rewarding ways to waste it!

Recipes Have Been Taste Tested And Approved
It took two of us to write this book. And while that may be kind of sad on one hand, on the other hand it means that for a recipe to make the cut – both of us had to think it was awesome. Plus, we've been honing our Trader Joe's skills for a decade now – so we've tried just about every item you can find in the store. We know what's good.

If You Don't Like A Recipe – You Can Get Your Money Back!

No, not from us – from Trader Joe's! Any item you try and dislike, you just bring back the packaging and your receipt. They'll refund you. However, having tried our own recipes many many times – we doubt this will ever happen to you. But, it's pretty amazing. I mean what other cookbook can make such a claim?!

Caprese Salad

Ingredients:
½ Pint Grape Tomatoes - $1.25
4 oz Ciliegine Fresh Mozzarella - $1.75
1oz (5-6 leaves) Basil - $1.08
2 tbsp Olive Oil - $0.21
2 tbsp Balsamic Vinegar - $0.13
Salt
Pepper

Cost Per Meal: $4.42 Cost Per Serving:
$2.21

How To Make It:
Take your mozzarella and cut it up so the pieces are the same size as the grape tomatoes. In a bowl, mix them together with the oil, vinegar and basil. Add salt and pepper to taste. Take a fork. Start eating.

Pro Tips:
• Use dried basil spice instead of cutting up the real deal yourself. A stitch in time...
• If you have toothpicks, then you have yourself an appetizer for parties!

Recommended Side:
¼ package Frozen Edamame - $0.42

Chimichurri Soup

Ingredients:
1 Bag Frozen Chimichurri Rice/Veggies mix -
$2.99
1 Can Black Beans - $0.89
1 Carton Tomato & Roasted Red Pepper Soup
- $2.79

Cost Per Meal: $6.64 **Cost Per Serving:**
$1.66

How To Make It:
Heat up the Chimichurri mix as directed on the
bag, but use a soup pot instead of a pan to
save on eventual cleanup time. When the mix
is hot, add in the drained can of black beans
and the entire carton of soup. Bring to a boil,
and you can even let it simmer for a few
minutes if you want to thicken it a bit.

Pro Tips:
• If you're looking to fill the soup out even
  more, add some shrimp or shredded
  chicken.

Recommended Side:
Hearty Bread - Sourdough Boule Whole Wheat
- $0.31 per slice

Gyoza Soup

Ingredients:
3 Tbsp TJ's Olive Oil - $0.31
1 Package Gyoza's
- Veggie - $3.79
- Chicken - $3.79
- Pork - $3.79
- Shrimp - $4.79
1 TJ's Mirepoix - $2.99
2 packages TJ's Low Sodium Chicken Broth - $3.98
1 Bag TJ's Baby Spinach - $1.99
1 tbsp TJ's Soy Sauce - $0.09
1 tbsp TJ's Toasted Sesame Oil - $0.29

Cost Per Meal (6 Servings): $13.44 Cost Per Serving: $2.24

How To Make It:
Put a medium to large soup pot on the stove and turn on the heat. Add some oil and saute the mirepoix. When the veggies are starting to look transparent, add the broth and bring it to a simmer.

While the broth is heating up, lightly brown the gyozas of your choice in a frying pan. When the broth is simmering, add in the spinach, soy sauce, sesame oil, and gyozas. Let it boil for a few minutes to really cook in the flavor.

Pro Tips:
- Add salt if you feel you'd like a tastier but less healthy soup.
- Add some cilantro in honor of Caleb Nichol

Recommended Side:
1 Slice Sourdough Boule Bread - $0.31

Chili Mac

Ingredients:
½ Can Turkey Chili with Beans - $1.00
1 Packet TJ's Microwaveable Mac and Cheese - $0.50
1 oz Light Shredded Mozzarella Cheese - $0.25

Cost Per Serving: $1.75

How To Make It:
Microwave one half can of turkey chili for approximately three minutes. Empty the macaroni into a bowl with one cup of water and microwave for 90 seconds. Combine turkey chili with macaroni and sprinkle 1 TBSP of cheese on top.

Pro Tips:
- The chili tends to splatter, so if you want to avoid a mess be sure to cover your bowl with a paper towel.

Recommended Side:
Guilt-Free Tortilla Chips - $1.99 per bag
Garlic bread - $1.99 per box

Easy Gallo Pinto
Note: this translates to Painted Rooster, but no paint or roosters are needed.

Ingredients:
1 cup cooked Basmati Rice - $0.75
1 Can TJ's Black Beans - $0.89
TJ's Pico De Gallo Salsa - $2.99

Cost Per Serving: $4.63

How To Make It:
Some people like microwaveable quick and easy rice. Some people like to start with dry rice and make it in a pot. We don't care what kind of rice person you are - just go ahead and make the rice per the directions on the package.

Open and drain the black beans. Mix together with the pico de gallo salsa in a microwaveable bowl. Then, microwave it until it's hot.

We like to just put the bean and salsa mix over the top of the rice, but you could also mix it all together if that's your thing.

Eat it and tell all your friends how Costa Rican your diet is.

Pro Tips:
- Scramble some eggs to eat with it - breakfast of champions!
- Add a little chicken to the mix - lunch of champions!

Add even more chicken to the mix - dinner of champions!
Eat it at midnight - midnight snack of champions!

Recommended Side:
Reduced Guilt Tortilla Chips and TJ's Guacamole - $1.50

Orange Chicken

Ingredients:
½ Bag TJ's Orange Chicken - $2.50
1 Pack Orange Chicken Sauce - $0.00
(included with Orange Chicken)
¼ Cup Basmati Rice - $0.19

Non-Mandatory Ingredients:
¼ Pack Melange-A-Trois (frozen peppers) -
$0.63

Cost Per Serving: $2.69 w/Peppers $3.32

How To Make It:
Preheat the oven to 400 degrees. Put half the bag of chicken onto a baking sheet and bake for 17 minutes, not the 20 minutes Trader Joe's asks for (they're so clueless). Like a champ you'll be cooking those last 3 minutes in a frying pan. Pour a glass of hot water and drop one of the orange chicken sauce packs in it to defrost. If you have slow rice, start it now.

When there's two minutes to go, if you're adding the optional Melange-A-Trois, start them peppers a-cooking in a frying pan on the stove (medium high). If you have fast cook rice, start it now.

When the 17 minute timer sounds, add the chicken to the frying pan. Pour in the now defrosted sauce. The frying pan should seer the sauce onto the chicken and peppers and cook in the flavor. Cook till the sauce is all fried up.

Throw your chicken and pepper over your rice and you have a 20 minute meal Trader Ming would be proud of.

Pro Tips:
- Line your baking sheet with tin foil, increases cost by a few cents, but decreases clean up time.
- FoodSaver the second half of your Orange Chicken bag along with the second sauce pack, 'cause nobody likes freezer burn.
- Add the peppers or your choice of TJ's veggies. Chicken and rice is for babies. Chicken, rice, and veggies is for men.

Recommended Side:
1 Trader Joe's Stir Fried Vegetable Egg Rolls - $0.74

Buffalo "Breaded Chicken" Wings

Ingredients:
4 Pieces of TJ's Breaded Chicken - $2.50
2 tbsp TJ's Habanero Hot Sauce - $0.71
1 tbsp Butter - $0.09
1 Ziplock bag - Really cheap

Cost Per Serving: $3.30

How To Make It:
Preheat oven and bake the chicken as per the directions on the bag. While the chicken is cooking, microwave the butter until melted.

Pour the melted butter into a ziplock bag. Add in the hot sauce. Your plastic bag should now look very unappetizing. But wait, there's more! When the chicken is done baking, add the chicken pieces to the ziplock bag. Seal it up (this is very important). Then shake it, shake, shake it, shake it, shake, shake it....

Pro Tips:
- Remember to fully seal the ziplock bag.
- If you're in a hurry, microwave the chicken for 3 minutes and 45 seconds
- To save the 2 cents a ziplock bag costs, you can do your mixing in a bowl. Note: this is not as fun.
- If you are ever in a non-Trader Joe's grocery store, buy Frank's Hot Sauce. We know, this is sacrilege - but it's really the ideal choice for that 'Buffalo Wing' flavor.

Recommended Side:

2 oz Ranch or Blue Cheese Dressing - $0.58
3 stalks Celery - $0.57
½ package Sweet Potato Fries - $1.15

Easy Oven Ribs

Ingredients:
1 Rack TJ's Baby Back Ribs - $8.50/lb
½ Bottle TJ's BBQ Sauce - $1.25
1oz Dry Rub (non TJ's item) ≈ $1.00
Tinfoil (Non TJ's Item) - Very Cheap

Cost Per Serving (Makes 2): $5.38

How To Make It:
Preheat the oven to 275. While that is happening, coat both sides of the ribs with the dry rub. Sometimes adding a little olive oil can help the process go a little more smoothly. Put the ribs on a baking sheet and cover the sheet with tinfoil to lock in the moisture.

Bake for an hour. Flip the ribs over. Re-secure the tinfoil, put back in the over. Bake for another hour. Take the ribs out. Turn the oven up to 350. Apply a light coat of BBQ sauce to the side facing up. Re-secure the tinfoil. Put the ribs back in the oven for 15 minutes.

After 15 minutes, take the ribs out. Flip them over. Apply a light coat of BBQ sauce. Re-secure the tinfoil. Bake for another 15 minutes.

Take the ribs out. Yer done!

Pro Tips:
- Experiment with different dry rubs and sauces until you find your perfect mix.

- Eat the whole rack in one sitting. Sure it's supposed to be two meals so you'll be uncomfortably full - but it's a really tasty uncomfortable feeling.
- Put a few onion slices on top and under the ribs while baking for bonus flavor.

Recommended Side:
TJ's Cornbread - $2.69 per package
Mashed Potatoes - $0.39 per potato

Polenta Provencale with Sausage (Gluten Free!)

Ingredients:
1 Bag Polenta Provencale - $3.69
1 Spicy Italian Vino & Formaggio Chicken Sausage - $1.00
A little water $0.00

Cost Per Serving: $4.69

How To Make It:
Fill up your frying pan with ¼ inch of water. Turn it on medium high. Add your sausage to start cooking it. Technically you could just fry up the sausage, but we find that this frequently results in burning the outside of the sausage and not fully cooking the interior. But the water prevents the burning, and when it starts to boil, it also helps cook the sausage faster. Keep rotating it, it'll probably take a little under 10 minutes to cook.

Remove the sausage and dump out the water. Put the pan back on the stove and start cooking the Polenta Provencale. While this is cooking, thin slice the sausage. Once the cheese has melted and is starting to cook down, toss in your sausage. Continue cooking all together until the cheese has been cooked into the pasta.

Pro Tips:
• You can use two pans and cook the sausage at the same time as the Polenta

Provencale, but then you'll have to wash twice as many pans!

- This is really good with an andouille sausage, but those aren't sold at TJ's.

Recommended Side:
Lentil Salad

Butter Chicken with Basmati Rice, Masala Tandoori Naan, and Samosas

Ingredients:
1 Pack Butter Chicken with Basmati Rice - $3.49
1 Piece Frozen Tandoori Naan - $0.57
2 Pieces Vegetable Samosas - $1.23

Cost Per Serving (sides already included!): $5.29

How To Make It:
Remove Butter Chicken from package and poke holes in the plastic cover. Put package on a baking sheet and place in oven. Cook as directed and set a timer for two minutes less than recommended. When the timer goes off add a piece of the naan to the baking sheet and continue cooking the Butter Chicken and Naan for the final two minutes.

Samosas. Put them in the microwave for 1:11 (we do this cause it's faster to just keep hitting the same button three times). While they are microwaving, heat up a pan on the stove to medium. Simply microwaving them makes them too soft, so just throw them in the pan for a half a minute or so on each side to crisp them up! Mmmmm.

Pro Tips:
- Buy Frozen Tandoori Naan instead of the fresh Masala Tandoori Naan since it tends to spoil quickly.

Recommended Side:
All the sides you need are in there!

Channna Masala with Chicken and Zucchini

Ingredients:
1 Package TJ's Channa Masala - $2.29
1 Chicken Breast - $1.20
1 Zucchini - $0.76
¼ cup TJ's Basmati Rice - $0.19

Cost Per Serving: $4.44

How To Make It:
Defrost the Channa Masala. It doesn't have to be totally defrosted, but you don't want to be working with a frozen brick. Start the rice and cook as directed.

Cut up the chicken breast into bite sized pieces and start cooking them up in the frying pan. Slice up the zucchini into thin pieces, and then cut those pieces in half. When the chicken is almost done, add the zucchini slices to the pan.

After the zucchini slices have had a few minutes to get cookin', add in the defrosted channa masala. Heat until hot. Serve over the rice you made!

Pro Tips:
- If you prefer the microwaveable rice, the brown rice is the better option here we think.

Recommended Side:
1 Piece TJ's Frozen Tandoori Naan - $0.57

Meat & Heat Pizza

Ingredients:
1 Pack TJ's Plain Pizza Dough - $1.19
4 oz TJ's Grilled Chicken Strips - $1.76
15 Slices o' Jalapenos (NOT SOLD AT
TRADER JOE'S) ≈ $0.50
4 oz TJ's BBQ Sauce - $0.56
1 Cup Light Shredded Mozzarella Cheese -
$2.66
1 Spray TJ's Canola Oil Cooking Spray -
$0.004

Cost Per Pizza: $6.674 **Cost Per Serving:**
$2.22

How To Make It:
Get the dough out of the fridge a little ahead of
time so it has time to warm up for optimal
stretchability. Preheat the oven as per the
package.

Spray a little cooking spray on the pan.
Carefully stretch the dough across the pan.
Poke a few holes in the dough with a fork to
avoid bubbling. Pre-bake the dough for 8
minutes - otherwise we find you'll end up with
doughy dough. Sick!

Take your pan back out of the oven and cover
the dough with a thin layer of BBQ sauce. Add
the chicken strips and jalapenos. Cover with
mozzarella.

Return the tray to the oven and bake it as
directed. When it finishes, let it sit for a few

minutes before you cut it. Otherwise that annoying thing will happen where the cheese gets pulled across the pizza by the pizza cutter and it will totally ruin the aesthetic you've created.

Pro Tips:
- It's cheaper if you buy uncooked chicken breasts, slice and cook them yourselves. It probably will taste slightly better, too. But, only real pro's are up for this challenge.
- Add more jalapenos

Recommended Side:
According to my elementary school, pizza should be served with canned corn. ½ Can - $0.89
1 Bag TJ's Caesar Salad Mix Bag - $3.99

Traditional Pizza

Ingredients:
1 Pack TJ's Whole Wheat Pizza Dough - $1.19
1 Cup TJ's Pizza Sauce (can) - $1.00
8 oz TJ's Mozzarella Cheese - $2.66
20 slices of TJ's Sliced Pepperoni - $0.83
1 Spray TJ's Canola Oil Cooking Spray - $0.004

Cost Per Pizza: $5.684 **Cost Per Serving:** $1.895

How To Make It:
Preheat the oven as directed. While it's preheating, take the dough out of the fridge - this will help with the dough spreading.

Spray your cookie sheet a little bit so that the pizza doesn't stick and the spreading goes smoothly. Spread the dough. Poke a few holes with a fork to prevent unsightly bubbles, then pre-bake the dough for about 8 minutes.

Take the cookie sheet back out 'cause now it's time to add the toppings. The order of operations is as follows: sauce, cheese, pepperoni. Only a fool, or people living in Chicago, would put the pepperoni under the cheese.

Bake the pizza as directed.

Pro Tips:
- You can replace the pepperoni with Trader Joe's sausages sliced up real thin-a-like.

- Get yourself a pizza stone, they really do improve the crust.

Recommended Side:
More pizza. When you have pizza with your pizza, you can have pizza anytime.

Pesto Chicken Pizza

Ingredients:
1 Pack TJ's Garlic & Herb Pizza Dough - $1.19
4 oz TJ's Grilled Chicken Strips - $1.76
1 Roma Tomato - $1.33
2 oz Mushrooms - $0.40
3 tbsp Pesto - $0.64
8 oz TJ's mozzarella cheese - $2.66
1 Cup Jar Trader Joe's Alfredo Sauce - $1.46
1 Spray TJ's Canola Oil Cooking - $0.004

Cost Per Pizza: $9.444 **Cost Per Serving:** $3.148

How To Make It:
Take the dough out of the fridge to warm it up, and preheat the directed temperature. While that's going on, wash, and then slice the roma tomato. If your mushrooms aren't already pre-sliced, slice'm now.

Spray your cookie sheet, and stretch the dough across it. Poke a few holes to prevent bubbling. Pre-bake the dough for 8 minutes. Trader Joe's doesn't say to do this on their package, but we think you should.

Take the dough out, and cover it with a very thin layer of alfredo sauce. Then, add some pesto and mix it into the sauce. Our 3 tbsp's of pesto was sort of a rough guideline - the real amount will depend on how delicious you want your pizza to be.

Add the chicken, tomatoes and mushrooms. Cover with cheese. Bake as directed.

Eat.

Pro Tips:
- Cooking and slicing a chicken breast yourself will save money, but add time.
- Twist and pull to remove the stem of the mushroom before slicing.
- Really wash the mushrooms well. Nobody likes fungus on their fungus.

Recommended Side:
1 Bag TJ's Caesar Salad Mix - $3.99

Mexican Pizza

Ingredients:
2 TJ's Flour Tortillas With Whole Wheat - $0.46
⅓ TJ's Salsa Jar - $0.76
½ Can TJ's Black Beans - $0.45
½ Can TJ's Canned Corn - $0.45
1 Chicken Breast - $1.20
½ TJ's Taco Seasoning Pouch - $0.40
½ Bag TJ's Shredded Mexican Cheese - $1.65
A little bit of water - $0.00

Optional Ingredients:
TJ's Guacamole - $3.99

Cost Per 2 Pizzas: $5.37 **Cost Per Serving:**
$2.685

How To Make It:
Preheat the oven to 425. While this is
happening, cut up your chicken breast into
small pieces and start cooking it up in a frying
pan over medium high heat. When it's pretty
close to being done, mix your taco seasoning
pouch up in a cup of water and add it to the
pan. Make sure all of the chicken gets
covered. Turn up the heat so the water will
cook down.

While the taco juice is cooking down, you can
focus on these next steps. Put your two
tortillas on a baking sheet and bake for 1
minute, flip, and bake for another minute. This
will help the tortillas start to be a little crisp -
which will mean they'll be perfectly crispy when

you get to the end! You should also open and drain the black beans and corn.

Now it's time to add the 'za ingredients. The salsa acts as your sauce, so spread that over the tortillas first. Then add black beans and corn, use about a quarter a can per pizza. Add your taco seasoned chicken. Then sprinkle your mexican cheese blend over the top.

Bake for 11 minutes. Remove from the oven and let cool for a minute or two before cutting into slices. For those of you who bought the optional (but recommended!) guacamole, now is the time to spoon a bit of the green stuff on top.

Pro Tips:
- Use the lid of the can to hold the beans/corn in place while you drain it. This might not really be a 'pro' tip, but just a tip.
- Spice up your night with a hot salsa.
- If no one else is around, it's ok to say 'Arriba Arriba' after you take your first bite.

Recommended Side:
Pizza is a total meal kind of food.

Pizzadillas

Ingredients:
2 TJ's Flour Tortillas with Whole Wheat - $0.46
20 Pepperoni Slices - $0.83
1 Cup Light Shredded Mozzarella Cheese - $2.66
⅙ Bag of Spinach - $0.33
1 Spray TJ's Canola Oil Cooking - $0.004
¼ Jar of Trader Giotto's Pizza Sauce - $0.50

Cost Per Serving: $4.784

How To Make It:
Spray a little canola oil on a frying pan. Place the frying pan on the stove and turn it up to low heat. Place one tortilla in the pan and flip it after approximately one minute. Put mozzarella cheese, pepperoni, and spinach on top of the tortilla and let sit. Once the cheese starts bubbling lift up one side of the tortilla with a spatula and flip it to close the tortilla in half. Remove the pizzadilla from the frying pan and serve.

While eating, dip it in the pizza sauce before taking bites. To heat the sauce, or to not heat the sauce - that is the question you'll have to answer for yourself.

Pro Tips:
- Really watch the tortilla closely to make sure it isn't burning.
- Folding it in half is trickier than you think - you don't want to lose any of those tasty toppings! Too slow and the toppings slide

down, too fast and you've got yourself a
catapult.

Recommended Side:
5 oz Apple sauce - $0.40
1 Piece String cheese $0.29

Pizza to Calzone Adaptation Guide

Ingredients:
Half the ingredients for any of our pizza recipes that are made with pizza dough.

Cost Per Calzone Equation = ((Cost of Pizza / 2)*1)/1 or ½ Cost of Pizza

How To Make It:
Remove the pizza dough from the fridge and separate in half. Return one half to the refrigerator while letting the other half sit for at least 20 minutes prior to using. Preheat the oven to 365.

Spray a cookie sheet and stretch the dough across it. Be sure to poke a few holes to prevent bubbling in the dough. Pre-bake for four minutes. This isn't on the dough instructions, but we think it's essential.

Remove the dough from the oven and put your ingredients onto half of the dough. Then pick up the other half so that it covers your toppings. Have the dough form a seal and put back in the oven for 12 minutes.

Pro Tips:
- We like to dip the calzone in a bowl of excess pizza sauce.
- Store the leftover dough in a tupperware container or FoodSaver bag.

Recommended Side:
None necessary!

Taco Salad

Ingredients:
1 lb Hamburger Meat - $2.69
1 Bag Lettuce - $1.29
½ Bag TJ's Tortilla Chips - $1.00
1 Can TJ's Black Beans - $0.89
1 Can TJ's Corn - $0.89
1 Pouch TJ's Taco Seasoning - $0.79
1 Pack TJ's Guacamole - $3.99
1 Jar TJ's Salsa - $2.29
1 Bag TJ's Mexican Cheese Blend - $3.29
Some Water - $0.00

Cost Per Meal (this serves 4): $17.12 **Cost Per Serving:** $4.28
*it's hard to save guacamole, so either have 3 friends over or be prepared to eat a lot of guac.

How To Make It:

Don't be fooled by the lengthy ingredient list, this meal is very easy to make.

Brown the hamburger meat and break it up into small, taco sized kernels. Drain the grease a few times while browning to promote health. When the meat is browned, add in a mug of water mixed with the taco seasoning, stir it around to get all the meat involved, and then turn up the heat so it starts cooking down. While that's happening--

Open and drain the beans and corn. Put them into separate bowls and microwave them for a little over a minute each to heat them up.

When the meat finishes, set up your taco salad like a pro. Put down some chips first, lettuce next, beans and corn, meat, salsa, cheese, guacamole. You're gonna like the way it tastes, I guarantee it.

Pro Tips:
- Use a chef's knife to chop up the already chopped lettuce into thin, small, taco salad sized pieces like you'd get at Taco Bell.
- Eat all the guacamole, it can't be saved.
- The rest of it is easy to save for leftovers, so it's a great way to have food for most of the week.

Recommended Side:
Are you joking? There's so much food in this food. You'll explode.

Tacos

Ingredients:
⅓ lb. 80/20 hamburger meat - $0.90
⅓ pouch TJ's taco seasoning - $0.26
¼ cup TJ's Shredded Mexican Cheese - $0.82
¼ cup TJ's salsa - $0.57
3 TJ's hard taco shells - $0.50
A little water - $0.00

Optional Ingredients:
⅓ can TJ's black beans - $0.30
1 oz Handful of TJ's Baby Spinach - $0.33

Cost Per Serving: $3.68

How To Make It:
Brown the hamburger meat in a frying pan, break it up into tiny pieces while this is happening. Remember to drain the grease! When the meat is cooked, add in a half mug of water mixed with the taco seasoning. Mix it around, and turn up the heat to start cooking down the liquid.

While the meat is cooking down, if you're using the optional black beans - now is the time to open, drain, and microwave them.

Otherwise, when the meat is taco-fied, just add the meat, salsa, cheese and any optional ingredients you're using into the shells! Simps.

Pro Tips:
- FoodSaver the taco seasoning pouch to avoid spills

- Jalapenos. They'll put hair on your chest and flavor in your tacos.

Recommended Side:
1 Can Refried beans - $1.09

Beefy Enchiladas

Ingredients:
5 TJ's Flour Whole Wheat Tortillas - $1.15
1 lb Hamburger Meat - $2.69
½ Pouch Taco Seasoning - $0.40
1 Can TJ's Black Beans - $0.89
½ Bag TJ's Shredded Mexican Cheese - $1.65
½ Jar Salsa - $1.15
¾ Bottle Enchilada Sauce - $1.72

Cost Per Meal: $9.65 **Cost Per Serving:** $1.93

How To Make It:
Preheat the oven to 400. While this is happening brown the hamburger meat in a frying pan. Drain the grease to prevent heart attacks. When the meat is browned, pour in a mug of water mixed with taco seasoning. Mix it up real good and turn up the heat to start the liquid cooking down.

While that's happening open and drain the can of black beans. Spray a little canola oil on the inside of a lasagna pan. No one likes enchiladas that rip in half when you serve them. Pour a little bit of enchilada sauce into the pan and spread it around with a spoon, just enough to cover the bottom with a very thin layer.

When the meat has boiled down, it's time to start assembling the enchiladas. We find that microwaving each tortilla before assembling helps prevent tears. One by one, fill the center strip (all the way from end to end) of the tortilla with meat, beans, salsa and cheese. Roll it in up and place it in the pan. We find that five enchiladas fill the pan up nicely and make for a good division of ingredients without having to skimp on any of the 'ladas.

When your pan is full, pour enchilada sauce over the whole nine yards. Make sure you get the sides. Spread it around with a spoon. Any unsauced areas of the tortilla will be crunchy. This. Is. The. Worst.

Sprinkle some more cheese over the top to make it look profesh, and then bake it in the oven for 15 - 20 minutes.

Pro Tips:
- Make sure you fill the tortillas end to end, otherwise you'll have just empty tortilla bites before you get to the good stuff.
- Double and triple check that your tortillas have been fully covered in enchilada sauce.
- Sprinkling sliced black olives over the top before you bake it is a pretty cool move, if you're into that sort of thing.
- Sometimes the tortillas can unfold in the pan. Lay a knife over the top to help keep them shut until you pour the enchilada sauce over the top and lock them in place.

Recommended Side:
¼ pack Chimichurri Rice - $0.75
Reduced Guilt Tortilla Chips and TJ's Guacamole - $1.50

Veggie Enchiladas

Ingredients:
5 TJ's Flour Whole Wheat Tortillas - $1.15
1/4 Pouch Taco Seasoning - $0.20
1 Can TJ's Black Beans - $0.89
1 Can TJ's Corn - $0.89
½ Bag TJ's Baby Spinach - $1.00
½ Bag TJ's Shredded Mexican Cheese - $1.65
½ Jar Salsa - $1.15
¾ Bottle Enchilada Sauce - $1.72

Cost Per Meal: $8.63 **Cost Per Serving:** $1.73

How To Make It:
Preheat the oven to 400 degrees. Add a little bit of water mixed with taco seasoning to a frying pan and turn it to medium heat. Throw in the spinach and cook it down until the water is absorbed. While this process is taking place, open and drain the beans and corn.

Line the bottom of a baking tray with enchilada sauce - not too much, just enough to cover it. Now it's time to start filling the tortillas. Microwave each tortilla for 15 seconds as you start the process to prevent tearing.

Fill the tortilla down the center strip, from end to end, with cheese, spinach, beans, corn and salsa. Then roll it up and place it in the lasagna pan. You should be able to fit at least five enchiladas in the pan comfortably. When the pan is full, pour enchilada sauce over the tops and spread it with a spoon. You want to make sure every part of the tortillas are covered in sauce, otherwise they'll burn. If you're feeling like really setting the mood, sprinkle some more cheese over the top and dim the lights.

Bake for 15-20 minutes.

Pro Tips:
- Sometimes those pesky tortillas can flop open in the pan while you're filling the next one. Um... ANNOYING! Just lay a knife over the top of them to hold them in place until you get to the saucing.
- Don't cook the spinach for too long, spinach is kinda like those plastic shrink toys you'd bake as a kid - so the more you cook it, the less you have. This may seem to contradict the first law of thermodynamics, but remember: spinach is not energy, unless you are Popeye.

Recommended Side:
¼ pack Chimichurri Rice - $0.75
Reduced Guilt Tortilla Chips and TJ's Guacamole - $1.50

Grape and Brie Quesadilla

Ingredients:
2 TJ's Flour Tortillas with Whole Wheat - $0.46
4 oz TJ's French Brie - $2.00
Enough Grapes to lightly cover a tortilla ≈ $1.00
1 Spray TJ's Canola Oil Cooking - $0.004

Cost Per Serving: $3.464

How To Make It:
Cut the brie into thin slices and chop the grapes in half. Set aside.

Spread a little canola oil on your frying pan. Turn the stove up to low heat and place your pan on the burner. Put one tortilla in the pan and flip it after approximately one minute. Add brie and grapes and let sit. Once the cheese starts bubbling lift up one side of the tortilla with a spatula and flip it to close the tortilla in half. Remove the quesadilla from the frying pan and serve.

Pro Tips:
- Really watch the tortilla closely to make sure it isn't burning.
- Folding it in half is trickier than you think - you don't want to lose any of those tasty toppings! Too slow and the toppings slide down, too fast and you've got yourself a catapult.

Recommended Side:
This food flies solo.

Pulled Pork/Chicken/Brisket Sammies

Ingredients:
Your Choice of BBQ Pulled Meat (each makes four servings)
¼ Package Chicken - $1.37
¼ Package Pork - $1.37
¼ Package Brisket - $1.50
1 Hamburger Bun - $0.31

Optional Ingredients:
2 oz TJ's Blue Cheese Dressing - $0.58
2 tbsp TJ's Habanero Hot Sauce - $0.71
1 slice TJ's provolone cheese - $0.37

Cost Per Serving (Chicken, Pork): $1.68
Cost Per Serving (Brisket): $1.81

How To Make It:
Basically there are two ways to prepare your roll/bun. The first method is for toasty buns. Use a grill pan or a conventional toaster to brown your bread as you see fit. While the toasting is commencing, heat up the pulled meat in the microwave for about a minute.

The second method is for the warm, soft bread lovers. In this case, put your pulled meat choice on the bread. Don't close it yet. Microwave your sandwich for a little over a minute.

The optional ingredients are for those looking for a little extra zing. Just coat the top of the bun with your choice of dressing or hot sauce or cheese.

Pro Tips:
- Trader Joe's doesn't sell jalapeno slices, but we think a little spice is nice. Sometimes we even call this sort of combo "meat and heat".
- FoodSaver the remaining meat for freshness.
- If you don't have a FoodSaver, tupperware is probably your best bet - you can leave the meat in the plastic bag it comes in. This saves time on tupperware cleanup.
- Store unused sandwich rolls in the freezer so that they keep longer.

Recommended Side:
¼ Bag TJ's BBQ Popped Chips - $0.50
½ Bag Sweet Potato Fries - $1.15
1.5 cups Apple Slices - $1.00

Chicken Parmesan Sandwich

Ingredients:
2 Pieces TJ's Breaded Chicken - $1.25
1 Hamburger bun - $0.31
1oz TJ's Shredded Parmesan Cheese - $0.42
1 Jar Trader Giotto's Tuscano Marinara Sauce
- $1.29

Cost Per Serving: $3.27

How To Make It:
Start by microwaving two pieces of TJ's
Breaded Chicken for 90 seconds. Remove the
chicken and sprinkle on the parmesan cheese.
Microwave the chicken and cheese combo for
another 90 seconds. Again remove the chicken
and add the marinara sauce to the top of it.
Microwave for 60 seconds and then put the
chicken parm concoction on one sandwich roll.

Pro Tips:
- Toast the sandwich roll on a grill pan or in a
  conventional toaster. Alternatively, you
  could throw the roll in the microwave for 30
  seconds or so.
- In a pinch, you can use TJ's Light Shredded
  Mozzarella Cheese for an equally delicious
  combination.
- As always, everything is more delicious with
  a few jalapeno slices on top.

Recommended Side:
1 Bag TJ's Caesar Salad Mix - $3.99
TJ's Asparagus Spears - $3.99

Hamburgers - A Few Thoughts Followed By Some Burger Brainstorms

When it comes to hamburgers, Trader Joe's has a TON of frozen patty options. Here's a quick rundown of the "fropat" (we just coined that term, don't steal it) options in order of goodness:

Kobe Beef - $1.50/patty
Chile Lime Chicken - $0.87/patty
Turkey Burgers - $0.75/patty
Salmon - $1.50/patty

But here's the thing with the frozen patties. They're good. They're super easy to make. And they're pretty cost effective. So if that's what you're looking for, by all means, knock yourself out. You're also gonna want to pick up some of the following (broken down into price by burger):

1 TJ's Hamburger Bun - $0.31
1 oz TJ's Ketchup - $0.08
1 slice Roma Tomato - $0.05
1 Piece of Lettuce $0.05
1 Slice of Onion $0.11

But let's cut to the chase. The frozen patties might leave you wanting. For a better burger, make the patty yourself out of ground hamburger meat. Or, if you're really cool. Get a meat grinder and grind up one of their steaks.

½ lb. TJ's 80/20 hamburger meat - $1.35

½ lb. TJ's Steak - $3.00

Once you've got your base of meat add in a touch of the following to fill it out:

1 oz Lea & Perrins Worchestershire Sauce - $0.20
1 oz TJ's Organic Bread Crumbs - $0.30
1 Egg (note: some people aren't all about this, but it does help hold the meat together while cooking) - $0.15

Much beyond that, if you're looking to try to add some creativity to your burgers. Here are a few easy ideas that we think you'll like. We're going to go ahead and assume that you're using the ½ lb. TJ's Hamburger Meat and 1 Bun. This will be known as 'Hamburger Starter Kit' in the ingredients.

The Goober Burger

Ingredients:
Hamburger Starter Kit - $1.66
2 tbsp of TJ's peanut butter - $0.17
1 slice Roma Tomato - $0.05
2 tbsp TJ's Mayo - $0.11

Cost Per Serving: $3.43

How To Make It:
Scoop a little bit of peanut butter into a bowl and microwave it for a few seconds to warm it up. After you've grilled your burger to the done-ness you like, add the peanut butter to the top bun. Add the mayo to the bottom bun. We know - mayo sends up a red flag for a lot of people, especially when we're asking them to pair it with peanut butter. We'd agree with those people if we hadn't already eaten these. Just try it! Put the tomato slice on top of your burger and get ready to rumble.

Pro Tips:
• Don't wuss out on the mayo

Recommended Side:
½ package TJ's Garlic Fries - $1.35
½ package TJ's Sweet Potato Fries - $1.15

The Blueberry Burger

Ingredients:
Hamburger Starter Kit - $1.66
Handful of blueberries - $0.75
2 oz TJ's Organic Blueberry Spread - $0.46

Cost Per Serving: $2.87

When you're mixing up your patty, mix the handful of blueberries into the meat. It may seem bizarre, but the sweet and savory combination will knock your socks off. Instead of ketchup, use the blueberry spread.

Take a bite. Then go find your socks.

Pro Tips:
- The blueberries won't save very long. So either make enough burgers to use them all, use them in another dish, or eat them by the handful.

Recommended Side:
½ package TJ's Garlic Fries - $1.35
½ package TJ's Sweet Potato Fries - $1.15

Pineapple Express Burger

Ingredients:
1 spear Trader Joe's Pineapple Spears - $0.58
¼ package TJ's Guacamole - $1.00
Hamburger Starter Kit - $1.66

Cost Per Serving: $3.24

How To Make It:
Nothin' too wild or crazy here. Cut up the pineapple spears into thin pieces and put them on top of your burger. Then use the guacamole instead of ketchup.

Pro Tips:
- Wear a lei

Recommended Side:
½ package TJ's Garlic Fries - $1.35
½ package TJ's Sweet Potato Fries - $1.15

As Directed Meals

Most cookbooks tell you how to cook things. Ha. Not this section, my friends. 'As Directed Meals' means you cook the elements as directed. "But wait!" you're surely crying, "what's the point of just telling me what to buy? Can't I decide for myself?"

No. No you can't. Well, you could. And while Trader Joe's does allow you to bring back items you don't like for a full refund - you still have to go through the drawn-out process of going to the store, buying items, eating something you hate (sick!), and then bringing it back. We're gonna cut out the (sick!) and the bringing it back parts. We've tried it all, and not only are we gonna tell you what's good - we're gonna tell you what other good things to eat it with so you end up with a great meal. Here's the breakdown of how that works:

Good + Good = Great

Got it? Also, it's good to remember that when traveling to Trader Joe's, D=RT (destination = real tasty). Ok. Let's get started.

Meals:

1. Indian Fares + Rice (1/4 cup) + Veggie Egg Roll. $3.06
(we recommend Jaipur Vegetables, Punjab Eggplant, and Punjab Choley)

2. 3 Pieces Bread Chicken + ¼ Bag BBQ Popped Chips + ¼ container of Cottage Cheese. $2.87

3. Vegetable Green Curry + 1 serving TJ's Grilled Chicken Strips + ¼ Cup Rice. $3.64 (Vegetable Panang Curry is also great)

Breakfast:
1. 1 piece Trader Joe's Sweet Apple Chicken Sausage + 1 slice Trader Joe's Low Fat French Toast $1.18
(we recommend microwaving both items for an even quicker breakfast)

2. 2oz Trader Joe's 100% Liquid Egg Whites + TJ's Light Shredded Mozzarella Cheese + Salt + Pepper $0.70
(microwave the combination in 45 second increments, stirring at each break)

3. Trader Joe's Breakfast Burritos + Trader Jose's Salsa Authentica OR Trader Joe's Habanero Hot Sauce $1.92 or $2.25
(microwave burrito for ⅓ of the recommended time, cut it into fourths, and then resume microwaving to ensure the burrito is completed heated all the way through)

Breakfast:

Quick Cinnamon Raisin Oatmeal

Ingredients:
TJ's Organic Oats & Flax Instant Oatmeal -
$0.44
Water - $0.00
1 pinch TJ's Cinnamon - $0.01
¼ cup TJ's Golden Raisins - $0.24
⅛ cup TJ's Almond Slivers - $0.37
1 tsp TJ's Brown Sugar $0.02

Cost Per Serving: $1.08

How To Make It:
Combine one package of the oatmeal in a
microwaveable bowl with water and heat in
microwave as directed. Stir in the cinnamon,
raisins, almonds, brown sugar, and serve.

Pro Tips:
- Adjust cinnamon/brown sugar ratio to taste.
- You can substitute 1 TBSP of TJ's Creamy
  Salted Peanut Butter in place of cinnamon
  and brown sugar to switch it up.

Recommended Side:
Brown Sugar Bacon - $1.62

Egg in a Frame

Ingredients:
1 piece of bread - $0.28
1 egg - $0.15
1 tbsp Butter - $0.09

Cost Per Serving: $0.52

How To Make It:
Put a frying pan on medium-low. Coat the bottom with butter to avoid sticking (and for flavor). Using a small cup or shot glass, remove a circle from the middle of the piece of bread. Put the bread into the pan, with the circle next to it. Crack an egg into the hole in the middle of the bread.

Cook until the bread is toasted on the down side, then carefully flip. Flip the circle, too. Continue until the other side is equally toasty. Cook times vary depending on how well done you like your eggs!

When you serve it up, it's a pretty cool to put the toasted bread circle back on top - kinda like a hat.

Pro Tips:
- Covering the pan while cooking can expedite the process and ensures the the egg is cooking as fast as the bread.
- The bigger the hole, the faster the egg cooks.
- TJ's Sourdough bread is the best bread to use. We don't even really like sourdough

bread that much otherwise, but in this case - it's awesome.

Recommended Side:
Any Fruit
Brown Sugar Bacon - $1.62
The Today Show - $0.00

Dunkin Donuts Big N' Toasty

Ingredients:
2 Pieces of Bacon - $0.73
1 Piece of American Cheese - $0.36
2 Eggs - $0.30
2 pieces of bread - $0.55

Cost Per Serving: $1.94

How To Make It:
Heat up a pan to medium. Put in two pieces of bacon. Everyone likes their bacon at a very particular level of crispiness, so keep flipping until you've reached yours. Remove the bacon and put in between two paper towels to absorb the grease.

Drain most, but not all of the grease in the pan, then return to the stove. Crack your eggs in. Yeah, we know this isn't the healthiest way to cook an egg. But the bacon grease makes the egg taste especially Dunkin' Donuts-y. While the eggs are cooking, put your two pieces of bread into your toaster.

Flip your eggs as per your personal preference for egg done-ness. Take your now toasted toast and put your slice of cheese on the bottom piece. Put the eggs on top of the cheese - for melting purposes. Then put the bacon on top of that and close it off with the top toast piece!

Pro Tips:
• Runny yolks are better than solid yolks.

- Double the bacon, double the fun.

Recommended Side:
A 2nd Big N' Toasty.

Waffle Berry Sandwich

Ingredients:
Two pieces TJ's Frozen Toaster Waffles - $0.50
2 tbsp TJ's Cream Cheese - $0.22
1 oz Fresh or frozen berries (blueberries, strawberries, raspberries) - $0.25

Cost Per Serving: $0.97

How To Make It:
Follow the prep steps on the waffle box for two waffles. Once ready, spread a serving of cream cheese on one of the waffles. Top with either fresh or frozen berries and cover with the other waffle.

Pro Tips:
- In a pinch, you can microwave the frozen waffles.
- If you are feeling fancy, mix the cream cheese and frozen berries together in a bowl before spreading on the waffles.

Recommended Side:
Brown Sugar Bacon - $1.62
2 Pieces TJ's Peppered Uncured Turkey Bacon - $0.60
1 Link TJ's Sweet Apple Chicken Sausage - $0.80

Almond Protein Shake

Ingredients:
8 oz TJ's Almond Milk (available in original, chocolate, vanilla, or unsweetened vanilla) - $0.42
Two scoops Trader Darwin's Whey Protein (chocolate or vanilla) - $0.80/serving

Cost Per Serving: $1.22

How To Make It:
Combine almond milk with protein and stir. Once combined, drink up!

Pro Tips:
• Shake it more than you think you need to. Otherwise... clumps.

Recommended Side:
a workout

Brown Sugar Bacon

Ingredients:
4 Slices TJ's Uncured Applewood Smoked
Bacon - $1.33
¼ Cup Brown Sugar - $0.29

Cost Per Serving: $1.62

How To Make It:
Preheat oven to 350°. Put the bacon on a
baking sheet. Sprinkle with brown sugar (don't
be stingy). Bake the bacon for 30 - 40 minutes
until it looks so good you just can't wait any
longer before eating it.

Pro Tips:
• More brown sugar = more flavor

Desserts:

Joe-Joe Truffles

Ingredients:
1 Pack TJ's Cream Cheese - $1.79
Joe-Joe's (TJ's brand oreos) - $2.99
TJ's Semi Sweet Chocolate Chips - $2.29

Cost Per Dessert: $7.07 (makes 48 truffles)
Cost Per Serving: $0.44

How To Make It:
Get out the cream cheese and let it soften for at least ten minutes. While you're waiting, finely crush approximately ¾ of the Joe-Joe's (should yield around four cups). Set aside one cup of the crushed Joe-Joe's and combine the remaining three cups with the cream cheese in a bowl. Mix together with your hands until the two ingredients are completely combined. Then roll the mixture into 48 one-inch truffle balls and set aside.

Put the chocolate chips in a microwaveable bowl. Microwave in 30 second increments, checking and stirring the chocolate each time. Once the chocolate is melted, put a few truffles in a bowl at a time. Use a fork to roll and coat the truffles in chocolate. Carefully pick up each truffle and let the chocolate drip back into the bowl. Set the truffles on a baking sheet and sprinkle the remaining crushed Joe-Joe's on top. Once finished dipping all the truffles, let them stand until firm. Store in your refrigerator.

Pro Tips:
- Crushing the Joe-Joe's can be a hassle. If you have a large ziploc bag, put the Joe-Joe's inside and use a rolling pin or potato masher to crush them.

Easy Peanut Butter Cookies

Ingredients:
1 cup TJ's Creamy Salted Peanut Butter - $1.40
1 cup TJ's Pure Cane Sugar - $0.87
1 tsp Rumford Baking Powder - $0.05
1 Egg - $0.15

Cost Per Dessert: $2.47 (Makes 24 Cookies)
Cost Per Serving: $0.31

How To Make It:
Preheat the oven to 350 degrees. Cream together the peanut butter and sugar in a bowl. We recommend hand stirring. And if you're not familiar with creaming, it basically means to combine two ingredients without over-mixing them. Add the baking powder and then beat in the egg until it is all well mixed.

Begin to roll the dough into quarter sized balls. You can make larger cookies, but it works better if they are small. Roll the balls into some spare sugar and then place on a baking sheet lined with parchment paper.

Bake for 8-10 minutes until the cookies feel coherent but are still a little on the soft side. Remove from the oven and let sit for 10-15 minutes.

Pro Tips:
- Parchment paper is a healthy option because it doesn't require you to grease the

pan. If you don't have any, you can use baking spray to prep the baking sheet.

Two Ingredient Chocolate Mousse (http://www.youtube.com/watch?v=g28-9NVUHj0)

Ingredients:
2 packages Le Noir Amer Caco - $5.98
½ cup water - $0.00

Cost Per Dessert: $5.98 (Serves 4) **Cost Per Serving:** $1.50

How To Make It:
Fill a mixing bowl with ice and cold water. Take a slightly larger mixing bowl and set it on top of the first bowl so that the large bowl is touching the ice. Set aside.

Add the chocolate and water to a medium-size pan and melt the combination over medium heat with occasional stirring. Transfer the mixture into the large bowl that is sitting on top of the ice/water. Immediately start whisking (preferably with a wire whisk) at a feverish pace until the mousse thickens. Be careful not to over-whisk or else the mousse with get grainy.

Immediately transfer to serving cups and eat ASAP. Makes two servings.

Pro Tips:
- If the mixture gets grainy, move it back to the pan and reheat it to start the process over. This happened to us during our first attempt.

No-Bake Berry Cheesecake

Ingredients:
8 Whole Crackers TJ's Honey Graham
Crackers - $1.50
3 Tbsp TJ's Unsalted Butter - $0.28
8 oz TJ's Cream Cheese at room temperature -
$1.79
1 Cup TJ's Ricotta Cheese - $1.75
2 Tbsp TJ's Clover Honey - $0.21
Pinch of Salt - $0.01
1 ½ cups Blueberries, Strawberries, or
Raspberries - $2.99

Optional Ingredients:
Sugar (1/4 cup) = $0.22

Cost Per Dessert: $8.53 (Serves 10) **Cost
Per Serving:** $0.85

How To Make It:
Melt the butter in the microwave and then
combine with the crushed graham crackers in
an 8 or 9 inch square pan to make the crust. It
should be about ¼ inch thick. Temporarily
store in the refrigerator.

In a separate bowl, combine the cream
cheese, ricotta, honey, salt, and optional sugar.
Use a whisk or hand mixer to blend until
smooth.

Remove the crust from the refrigerator and
pour the cheese mixture on top of it, being
careful to pour it in evenly since it's difficult to
smooth over without lifting up parts of the crust.

Top the cheesecake with your favorite berry (if using strawberries, slice them up first). Toss in the refrigerator for an hour or so to let it set. Cut and serve!

Pro Tips:
- For some folks, the cheesecake might not be sweet enough, that's why we mention the optional inclusion of sugar.
- If you don't feel like crushing the graham crackers, you can use a pre-made graham cracker crust found at just about any regular grocery store.
- If using strawberries, try including some chocolate chips on the top for a sweeter cake.

Banana Roll-Ups

Ingredients:
1 package TJ's Flattened Bananas - $1.29
2 tbsp of TJ's Creamy Salted Peanut Butter - $0.17
or
2 tbsp of TJ's Cocoa Almond Spread - $0.31
Toothpicks

Cost Per Dessert: $1.46-$1.60 (Serves 4)
Cost Per Serving: $0.37-$0.40

How To Make It:
Lay the flattened strips of banana on a flat surface. Spread your desired portion of peanut butter or almond spread on the banana. Roll up and secure with a toothpick. Serve asap!

Pro Tips:
• We like to heat up our peanut butter before applying it to the banana, but it's not necessary.

Banana Boats

Ingredients:
1 Banana - $0.19
2 oz TJ's Semi Sweet Chocolate Chips - $0.38
2 tbsp of TJ's Creamy Salted Peanut Butter -
$0.17

Non-TJ's-Ingredients:
10 Mini Marshmallows - $0.20
Tinfoil - Really Cheap

Cost Per Serving: $0.74

How To Make It:
Preheat your oven to 350 degrees. Line a baking sheet with tinfoil and place the unpeeled banana on top of it. Make a slice down the length of the banana, but don't cut all the way through. Remove the cut section.

Line the gap with peanut butter. Place the marshmallows in the opening of the banana along with the chocolate chips. Loosely seal the foil along the side and top of the banana. Bake for 15 minutes. When finished, eat with a spoon straight from the banana.

Pro Tips:
• It's easier if you buy mini marshmallows at a different grocery store.

The End

Acknowledgements

We'd like to thank our parents, Theo Albrecht, Joe Coulombe, Mike Keft, Ross McNamara, Trader Ming, and you.

Non-TJ's-Acknowledgements

We would also like to thank jalapeños and tinfoil.

Pro Tips

"A real man creates his own luck." – Billy Zane, *Titanic*

"The worst part of public transportation is the public." – Darkwing Duck, *Darkwing Duck*

You're still here? It's over! There is no more.
Go to Trader Joe's. Go do something else. Just
put the book down, we don't have anything
else to say to you.

5553315R00046

Made in the USA
San Bernardino, CA
11 November 2013